Original title:
Friendship's Flame

Copyright © 2024 Swan Charm
All rights reserved.

Author: Swan Charm
ISBN HARDBACK: 978-9916-86-674-0
ISBN PAPERBACK: 978-9916-86-675-7
ISBN EBOOK: 978-9916-86-676-4

Flames that Bind

In the dark, two sparks ignite,
Dancing shadows, hearts take flight.
Whispers soft, secrets shine,
In the warmth, our souls entwine.

Fingers brush, a gentle trace,
In the glow, we find our place.
Promises deep, like steady fire,
Carving dreams, lifting higher.

Through the night, the embers glow,
Guiding paths, where love may flow.
Together strong, we face the storm,
In each other, we find our warmth.

As the dawn begins to break,
In our hearts, the world we make.
With every touch, we redefine,
In the light, our fates align.

Together we will always stand,
Fires linked by fate's own hand.
Let the flames, our spirits bind,
In this warmth, true love we find.

Warmlight Connections

In the twilight's soft embrace,
Familiar smiles, a sacred space.
Laughter lingers, hearts in tune,
Underneath a glowing moon.

Paths converge, like rivers blend,
In shared moments, we transcend.
Eyes meet, a spark ignites,
Guided by the stars' delights.

Whispers echo in the night,
With each story, purest light.
Hands entangled, fears dissolve,
In our warmth, we both evolve.

Through the chaos, life will spin,
In our hearts, the strength within.
Trust we build, like woven thread,
In every word, love's song is said.

As the seasons come and go,
New chapters write what we both know.
In every hug, a truth revealed,
In warm connections, souls are healed.

The Warmth We Share

In the glow of twilight's embrace,
Our laughter dances in the air.
Each story weaves a gentle lace,
With every smile, we find our share.

Hand in hand, we walk the line,
Moments cherished, hearts laid bare.
Through the storms, our spirits shine,
Together, facing all we dare.

The warmth ignites, a steady flame,
Binding us through joy and strife.
In this dance, we'll stake our claim,
Our love, the canvas of our life.

As stars emerge in the vast dome,
We find our peace in the night air.
With you, I know I am at home,
In the warmth that we both share.

Ember Reflections

Beneath the charcoal sky we sit,
Where embers flicker, whispers flow.
Each glowing spark a silent wit,
Reflecting dreams in softening glow.

The firelight dances on our skin,
Filling the void with tales untold.
In every flicker, new worlds begin,
In the warmth, our fears unfold.

We gather close like tender leaves,
As shadows play and stories weave.
In the stillness, the heart believes,
That out of tempest, we can cleave.

Our eyes ignite in glowing cheer,
An ember's tale, a shared delight.
In this moment, so vivid, so near,
Reflections gleam, our spirits bright.

Dancing with Flames

In the heart of the fire, we sway,
Whirling in rhythms, pure and free.
Each flicker inspires our play,
As flames beckon, we come to be.

With laughter soaring like the sparks,
We twirl beneath the starry skies.
In the night, we leave our marks,
As fervent heat ignites our sighs.

Each ember whispers secrets bold,
In tempest's breath, we find our grace.
Through stories warm and futures told,
We dance with flames, our hearts embrace.

With every spin, our spirits rise,
Caught in the magic, wild and bright.
In the glow, beneath moon's eyes,
We lose ourselves in pure delight.

A Beacon in the Night

In darkest hours, a light appears,
A beacon shining through the haze.
With every flicker, calm our fears,
Guiding us through the winding maze.

Its warmth draws near, a tender hand,
Illuminating paths unknown.
With courage found, together stand,
In the glow, we're never alone.

The night may fall, but hope ignites,
In every heart, a spark remains.
Through shadowed doubts, we seek the sights,
While love endures, through all terrains.

A vessel strong, our spirits soar,
As waves of light wash over me.
In the darkness, we find what's more,
A beacon's warmth, our legacy.

Glow of Affection

In the quiet of night,
Stars softly gleam bright,
Whispers of warmth fly,
Wrapped in love's light.

Beneath the moon's gaze,
Promises we trace,
Each heartbeat a song,
In this gentle space.

Hands entwined, we stand,
Time slips through our hand,
Like grains of warm sand,
In our dreamland.

With every embrace,
We find our own place,
A haven where hearts,
Forever embrace.

In the glow we share,
Love's tender, sweet flare,
Every moment a gift,
In this drifting air.

Sparks in the Silence

In the hush of the night,
A spark ignites bright,
Two souls start to dance,
Caught in chance's trance.

Silent words exchanged,
Emotions unchained,
The world fades away,
In this soft ballet.

Every glance holds fire,
A burning desire,
In the stillness found,
Our hearts' echo sounds.

With each quiet pause,
Unspoken because,
The universe spins,
As our love begins.

In the dark we see,
A flickering spree,
Sparks that light the way,
To a brand new day.

Flickering Trust

In shadows that play,
Doubts drift far away,
A bond forged in fire,
Stronger than desire.

With every small step,
We promise and prep,
A journey so true,
Built on me and you.

In laughter, we find,
Pieces of our mind,
Flickers of the light,
Guiding us through night.

With open hearts wide,
We let love decide,
Together we'll grow,
In faith's gentle flow.

Through storms we will sail,
Together prevail,
In trust, we will rise,
Under sparkling skies.

Hearts Alight

In the warm embrace,
We find our own place,
Hearts ignited bright,
Chasing dreams of light.

With laughter we glow,
In rivers we flow,
Every moment we steal,
Turns into a reel.

In whispers so sweet,
Our pulses do beat,
An orchestra's tune,
Underneath the moon.

As stars light the skies,
Reflected in eyes,
Together we'll soar,
To love's distant shore.

With hearts intertwined,
A legacy signed,
In this dance of two,
I'll always choose you.

Ties that Illuminate

In the quiet of the night,
Soft whispers take their flight.
Hearts connected, shining bright,
Love's warmth is pure delight.

Memories weave through the air,
With each moment that we share.
Laughter dances, dreams laid bare,
In this bond, we find our care.

Like stars that glimmer and glow,
Guiding paths that we both know.
Together through the ebb and flow,
Our ties strengthen, ever so.

In the twilight's gentle hue,
Every heartbeat brings us new.
In this dance, just me and you,
A tapestry of love rings true.

With each thread that binds our hearts,
Every journey, every start.
Faith and trust, the finest arts,
In this life, we play our parts.

Under the Candlelight

Flickering flames cast warm glow,
Secrets shared in twilight flow.
Whispers dance, feelings grow,
Under the candlelight's show.

Shadows play upon the walls,
Echoes of our gentle calls.
In this moment, time stalls,
As the night around us sprawls.

Eyes that meet, spark of grace,
Every glance, a soft embrace.
In this still, enchanted space,
We find solace, love's own trace.

Dreams entwined in flicker bright,
Holding hands through velvet night.
In this glow, all feels right,
Guided by love's pure light.

As the candle slowly wane,
Moments cherished, never vain.
In our hearts, love's sweet refrain,
Forever blooming, free from pain.

Fireflies in Sync

In the fields where shadows creep,
Fireflies weave a dance so deep.
Each flicker a promise to keep,
In their glow, our secrets seep.

Nighttime whispers, soft and sweet,
Nature's rhythm guides our feet.
Hearts aligned, our souls compete,
As fireflies in sync, we meet.

Laughter twinkles in the dark,
Lighting paths with every spark.
In this magic, we embark,
Painting skies with love's own arc.

Moments captured, swift and bright,
Like the stars, we share our light.
In this dance, we find our flight,
Bound together, pure delight.

As the dawn begins to rise,
Still we chase those glowing skies.
In our hearts, the fireflies,
A memory that never dies.

Light Through the Shadows

In the depths where darkness lies,
Hope emerges, never dies.
With each step, the spirit flies,
Finding light through shadowed skies.

Whispers echo in the night,
Guiding us toward the right.
In this journey, hearts take flight,
Yearning for that spark so bright.

Every challenge brings its test,
Yet together, we are blessed.
In each trial, we find rest,
Through the shadows, we are zest.

Light will pierce the dimming haze,
Turning gloom to brighter days.
In love's warmth, we softly blaze,
Chasing dreams in endless ways.

As the sun begins to rise,
Hope's reflection, in our eyes.
Through the shadows, we will rise,
Finding strength as love replies.

Kindles of Kinship

In the warmth of shared smiles,
We gather like stars at night.
Silent bonds intertwine,
Hearts ignite with gentle light.

Through laughter and whispered dreams,
We weave a tapestry rare.
Each thread a story gleams,
In the fabric of care.

Across time and rolling hills,
Our paths spark a dance so true.
In echoes, each spirit thrills,
Forever entwined, me and you.

In storms, we stand as one,
Shielded by love's embrace.
From challenges, we've not run,
In unity, we find grace.

Together, our spirits rise,
Beneath the vast, open skies.
We kindle, we share, we soar,
In kinship, we ever explore.

The Fire of Us

In twilight's glow, we spark,
Embers dance in the dark.
Fires burn with a fierce sigh,
Passions weave through the sky.

With whispered words, we stoke,
The flame that never chokes.
It flickers, it brightly shines,
In the depths of love's designs.

Each gaze, a flame's embrace,
In shadows, we find our place.
Together, we feed the heat,
In the rhythm of our beat.

Through the night, we share light,
In comfort, we find our sight.
Fire of connection burns,
In the heart, the world turns.

As dawn breaks, our fire glows,
In the warmth, true love knows.
We carry the spark ahead,
In the journey we will tread.

The Luminescent Loop

In circles where thoughts collide,
We shine, as we seek and guide.
Around and around we go,
In the light, our spirits grow.

Each laughter echoes within,
A connection deep and thin.
We loop in the dance of fate,
In the bright we celebrate.

Hands held, we form a ring,
In trust, we dare to sing.
A melody shared and bright,
In the strength of our light.

The moments, like stars, align,
In this loop, our hearts entwine.
We travel the paths unseen,
In a bond that's evergreen.

Together, we weave our tale,
In this wondrous, shining sail.
The loop holds our dreams so near,
In unity, we persevere.

In the Company of Light

In shadows, we find our grace,
Illumined by love's embrace.
With every step, we ignite,
In the company of light.

Together, we chase the dawn,
As night slowly fades and yawns.
With whispers, our hopes take flight,
Guided by the stars so bright.

Each moment, a beacon shines,
In the journey, love entwines.
Through trials that test our might,
We stand strong in the light.

As dreams swirl like petals fall,
We rise, and together call.
In echoes, we claim our right,
In the company of light.

Every heartbeat, a spark anew,
In this bond, we share our view.
Side by side, we conquer the night,
Forever bound in this light.

Hearthside Whispers

In the quiet night, we share,
Softly glowing, hearts laid bare.
Stories told by firelight's gleam,
In these moments, we dare to dream.

Warmth envelops, shadows dance,
In the silence, a sweet romance.
Every whisper, a thread we weave,
In this love, we truly believe.

The crackle sings of souls entwined,
Each flicker, a memory defined.
Through joyful laughter, through the tears,
In this haven, we conquer fears.

Hearthside shadows, secrets kept,
Under the stars, our dreams adept.
Together here, we find our peace,
In this bond, our worries cease.

As dawn breaks, the embers fade,
Yet in our hearts, the warmth won't jade.
Together always, through thick and thin,
In hearthside whispers, our lives begin.

Bonds of Radiance

Like stars that fill the velvet night,
Our connection glows, a brilliant light.
Heartbeats synchronized in time,
In every glance, a silent rhyme.

We stand together, side by side,
In every struggle, our hearts collide.
The warmth we share ignites the way,
Guiding us through both night and day.

Laughter echoes in the air,
In each moment, we show we care.
A tapestry of dreams we chase,
In this bond, we find our place.

Footprints left on shifting sand,
Together facing what life planned.
With every challenge, we take flight,
In the glow of love, we shine bright.

In the heart of darkness, we will stand,
With bonds of radiance, hand in hand.
The stars above, our only guide,
Together forever, we will abide.

The Glow of True Connection

Two souls converge, in silent grace,
In every meeting, a warm embrace.
The glow between us, soft and bright,
A beacon shining through the night.

With every word, a spark ignites,
In laughter shared, our joy takes flight.
Through whispered dreams and tender sighs,
In this glow, our spirit flies.

As seasons shift and time moves on,
The light we share remains our dawn.
Through thick and thin, we stand as one,
In every shade, our hearts are spun.

In mirrored reflections, we find truth,
In every moment, the essence of youth.
A melody that forever sings,
In the glow of our true connections' wings.

Hand in hand, through storms we steer,
With every heartbeat, loud and clear.
In this embrace, we find our way,
The glow of love will never sway.

Unity in the Dark

When shadows creep, and fears unfold,
In the dark, our hands we hold.
With whispered hopes, we light the way,
Together strong, come what may.

In silence shared, we find our ground,
In every heartbeat, a love profound.
Through trials faced, side by side,
In unity, we shall abide.

As night descends, we stand as one,
With every battle, we have won.
No fear can dim this light we share,
In unity, we conquer despair.

Together we tread this winding road,
With every step, we lift the load.
In the darkest hour, we are the spark,
A testament to love in the dark.

For when the world outside feels cold,
In our embrace, warmth unfolds.
With every heartbeat, we leave a mark,
In unity, we rise from the dark.

The Glow of Tomorrow

In the dawn's soft embrace, we rise,
Dreams alight beneath brightening skies.
Whispers of hope in the morning glow,
Each step we take, together we grow.

With shadows fading, fears drift away,
In unity, we find strength each day.
The future shines with endless waves,
A path of light where courage paves.

Through challenges faced, hand in hand,
We build the trust where love can stand.
With every heartbeat, a promise made,
In moments shared, our dreams cascade.

Together we dance in the gleam of fate,
In laughter and joy, we celebrate.
The glow of tomorrow, forever bright,
Guiding our journey, our shared delight.

A Bond Illuminated

In the quiet night, our spirits unite,
Two hearts entwined, igniting the light.
With every glance, a story is told,
A bond illuminated, precious as gold.

Laughter and warmth, a delicate thread,
We weave through the moments, our fears shed.
In the glow of trust, our spirits take flight,
Together we shine, like stars in the night.

Through storms we weather, side by side,
In the heart's deep chamber, love will abide.
Each challenge a chance to grow even stronger,
In the dance of our bond, we linger longer.

With gentle touches, we both heal,
In the sacred space, our souls reveal.
With every heartbeat, a promise we make,
Our bond illuminated, never to break.

Stars in our Eyes

In the midnight sky, when dreams ignite,
We chase the stars, our spirits in flight.
With hope as our compass, we venture afar,
Guided by love, like a shining star.

Through the vastness of night, we laugh and play,
Counting the wishes we cast each day.
With every heartbeat, our stories entwine,
Together we sparkle, like diamonds that shine.

In moments of silence, our hearts beat loud,
A universe shared, we stand, proud.
The galaxies whisper, our souls in sync,
In the depth of love, we find the link.

With our eyes turned up, we reach for the sky,
In the wonder of dreams, we learn to fly.
Stars in our eyes, a map to our fate,
In the dance of the cosmos, we patiently wait.

United by Warmth

In the hearth's embrace, where comfort reigns,
We gather together, shedding our chains.
With laughter like fire, our spirits will bloom,
United by warmth, we banish the gloom.

Each moment a treasure, each smile a spark,
In the heart's favorite place, love leaves its mark.
Through seasons that change, we stand resolute,
Together we flourish, our roots in pursuit.

In stories shared, our journey unfolds,
With memories cherished, our love is bold.
The warmth of connection, a sweet, gentle tide,
With hands interwoven, we stand side by side.

As daylight fades and twilight appears,
In the glow of our bond, we conquer our fears.
In the dance of our lives, we find our own way,
United by warmth, come what may.

The Heat of Togetherness

In the warm glow we find,
Hearts entangled like vines,
Laughter fills the air,
Love deepens and shines.

Side by side we stand,
Facing storms and the sun,
With each whispered dream,
Together we run.

Our hands clasped so tight,
A fortress built of hope,
Through nights dark and long,
Together we cope.

Every glance we share,
Ignites a spark so bright,
In the heat of love's fire,
We dance in the light.

As time travels on,
We weave futures anew,
In the heat of togetherness,
I am home with you.

Flickers of Trust

In the quiet of night,
A whisper lingers near,
Eyes meet across the room,
Allowing us to steer.

Flickers of trust arise,
In every gentle touch,
With each heartbeat we share,
It means so very much.

Through shadows we walk,
Fears slowly fall away,
In this fragile moment,
We find our own way.

As secrets come alive,
And stories start to blend,
Flickers of trust ignite,
On you I can depend.

With every word we speak,
Boundaries disappear,
In this dance of trust,
I'm grateful you are near.

The Bright Side of Us

In the morning glow,
We greet the rising sun,
With laughter in our hearts,
The day has just begun.

Moments shared like gold,
In every smile and glance,
Together we create,
A sweet, eternal dance.

Through trials and through tears,
We hold on to the light,
Finding joy in chaos,
Making wrongs turn to right.

With a spark in our eyes,
We chase away the gray,
The bright side of us shines,
Lighting up the way.

So here's to our journey,
Hand in hand we will go,
Embracing every turn,
Together we will grow.

The Warm Embrace

In the hush of twilight,
Arms wrap around me tight,
In this warm embrace,
Everything feels right.

The world fades away,
As we sway to the night,
In your arms I find peace,
A comfort, pure delight.

With whispers of love,
And gentle, soft sighs,
Moments swell like waves,
Underneath starlit skies.

Every heartbeat echoes,
With promises so true,
In this warm embrace,
I find my home in you.

So let the night linger,
As we hold on so close,
In the warmth of this love,
You are what I treasure most.

The Light Between Us

In the quiet whispers of the night,
Stars twinkle softly, hearts take flight.
A gentle glow that fills the space,
Together we shine, a warm embrace.

Through the shadows, our dreams align,
Guided by love, a celestial sign.
Hand in hand, we walk that line,
The light between us, forever divine.

In moments shared, tight and close,
The world fades, yet love engrossed.
Eyes that speak what words can't say,
In this glow, we lose our way.

Facing storms, we stand as one,
The battles fought, the victories won.
In every struggle, a spark remains,
A beacon bright, through joy and pain.

So here's to us, our hearts aglow,
In this haven where love does grow.
The light between us, pure and true,
Forever shining, me and you.

Bonds That Glow

In the tapestry of time we weave,
Threads of warmth, hopes we believe.
Every moment, a stitch anew,
A bond that glows, a love so true.

Through trials faced, we find our strength,
Together we'll travel any length.
In laughter shared and tears we shed,
This glowing bond, where all is said.

Every heartbeat a rhythmic song,
Together in this dance, we belong.
The whispers soft, the laughter loud,
In our hearts, we are so proud.

As twilight falls, a golden hue,
We chase the stars, just me and you.
In every glance, the spark ignites,
A bond that glows through starry nights.

So let us cherish all we know,
In this journey, our spirits flow.
With every passing day we grow,
In this embrace, our bonds that glow.

Embers of Togetherness

In the flicker of a dying flame,
Embers dance, yet still the same.
They flicker bright, though shadows loom,
Together we find warmth in gloom.

When the winds of change blow cold,
Our hearts are flames, brave and bold.
With every whisper, the embers flare,
Binding us close in love's sweet air.

In quiet moments, sparks ignite,
Illuminating even the darkest night.
These embers tell of stories shared,
A testament to how much we've cared.

Through every trial, we hold the light,
In this togetherness, we find our might.
The glow of love, a radiant thread,
In the tapestry where our dreams are fed.

So let us nurture this fire inside,
With every moment, let's take pride.
Embers of togetherness softly glow,
In this warmth, forever we'll flow.

Warmth in Solitude

In the quiet moments, peace we find,
Warmth in solitude, a gentle bind.
With every breath, the stillness speaks,
A haven for hearts, no need for fleets.

The world outside may rush and race,
Yet in this solitude, we embrace grace.
In whispers soft, we hear the call,
The warmth that rises, uniting all.

Lonely nights turn into dreams,
Where echoes dance in moonlit beams.
This solitude, our sacred space,
In every heartbeat, we find our place.

With every star that lights the sky,
We gather strength, we learn to fly.
In these moments, we come to see,
The warmth around, just you and me.

So let us treasure the silence shared,
In this solitude, we are prepared.
The warmth we nurture will ever grow,
In every heart, a soft, warm glow.

Dancing in the Firelight

Flickering flames leap high,
Casting shadows on the ground,
Laughter mingles with the night,
Hearts in joyful rhythms bound.

Warmth envelops every soul,
As we twirl in soft embrace,
The night's magic takes control,
Time suspends in this sweet place.

Stories whispered by the fire,
Echoes of the days gone by,
Every spark ignites desire,
Underneath the starry sky.

With the night, our spirits soar,
Feeling free just like the breeze,
Each moment we cannot ignore,
Lost in love, we find our peace.

As embers fade, we linger on,
In the glow of what we've made,
Through the night and into dawn,
In the memories that won't fade.

Together We Shine

In the tapestry of stars,
We find a path illuminated,
Side by side, despite the scars,
Our hearts are beautifully mated.

Every glance a promise shared,
In this world of vast unknown,
With each step, we feel prepared,
In our strength, we have grown.

Hands entwined, we face the dark,
Together facing every storm,
In the silence, we'll leave a mark,
A bond that keeps our hearts warm.

Through the valleys deep and wide,
We rise up, unafraid to climb,
With love as our steady guide,
We write our story, line by line.

In the light of every dawn,
We carry dreams, our spirits high,
Together we have always drawn,
A future where we both can fly.

Glow of Endurance

In the shadows of the night,
We stand firm, refusing to yield,
Through the trials, we find light,
In our hearts, a glowing shield.

Every moment, every sigh,
Builds a fire that will not fade,
With each heartbeat, we comply,
In this journey we have made.

Night may come with chilling fears,
But we rise, unbowed, unbroken,
Through the laughter and the tears,
In our love, the words unspoken.

Echoes of the battles won,
Filling us with strength anew,
In the dark, we are as one,
A resilient light shining through.

With each day that we embrace,
We carry hope, fierce and rare,
In the glow of our grace,
We rise up, vibrant as the air.

Lights of Resilience

Amidst the chaos and the strife,
We gather hope like scattered seeds,
In the gardens of our life,
We nurture strength that always leads.

Beneath the weight of heavy skies,
Our light emerges, fierce and bright,
With every challenge, we arise,
Fighting shadows with our might.

Each setback shapes our song anew,
A melody of brave persistence,
In unity, we're never through,
Our spirits dance with resistance.

Stars may flicker, yet they shine,
Reminders of what we can be,
In the darkness, we define,
The lights of our infinity.

Together, facing what may come,
In our hearts, a vibrant stream,
Resilience pulses like a drum,
Guiding us to reach our dream.

Glow of Kindness

In a world where shadows play,
A gentle light will find its way.
A smile shared, a hand held tight,
Kindness glows, a beacon bright.

In whispers soft, a heart can mend,
With every word, we love, we send.
A spark ignites, a flame anew,
Together, we will see it through.

In the laughter, in the tears,
Kindness echoes through the years.
Each little act, a glowing thread,
We weave our tapestry ahead.

When hope feels lost in darkest night,
A touch of kindness can ignite.
With every gesture, every deed,
The world can heal from pain and greed.

So let us shine, both near and far,
Guiding others like a star.
In the glow of kindness true,
A brighter day will follow through.

The Hearth of Souls

In a quiet room where shadows dance,
Hearts gather close, a sacred chance.
Stories told by flickering light,
The hearth of souls shines warm and bright.

With every laugh, a bond is made,
In the glow, our fears do fade.
A circle wide, embracing all,
Together strong, we will not fall.

Through trials shared, through joys we find,
The hearth of souls, forever kind.
In whispers low, truths take their flight,
We share our burdens, turn to light.

When the world feels cold and gray,
Let love's warmth light up the way.
In this space, we're never alone,
The hearth of souls, our cherished home.

So gather 'round, let spirits rise,
Each heart reflects the other's skies.
In unity, we're reborn whole,
United here, the hearth of souls.

Illuminating Journeys

Every path we choose to tread,
Holds a story yet unsaid.
With every step, a chance to grow,
Illuminating journeys flow.

In winding roads, through ups and downs,
Adventure calls, it wears no frowns.
Each moment rich, a lesson learned,
With every corner, passion burned.

Beneath the stars, our dreams take flight,
Guided softly by the night.
Horizons stretch with hope so bright,
Illuminating journeys ignite.

Through mountains high and valleys low,
In every heartbeat, life will flow.
We find our pace, embrace the yearn,
In every twist, a page we turn.

So take my hand, let's leap ahead,
With courage found, no fears to dread.
In this dance of life, we'll sway,
Illuminating journeys stay.

Together in the Dark

In shadows deep, where whispers creep,
We gather close, our secrets keep.
Fear may linger, doubt may spark,
But we stand firm, together in the dark.

Holding hands, we share our dreams,
Through troubled times, we're stronger teams.
A light ignites within our hearts,
Together brave, though night imparts.

With every step, we forge ahead,
In silent strength, where hope is fed.
Through trials faced, we claim our mark,
Together bold, together in the dark.

With every tear, we find the grace,
To lift each other, find our place.
In unity, we spark a flame,
A bond of trust, we're not the same.

So journey on, through thick and thin,
In every loss, a chance to win.
With hearts aligned, we leave our mark,
Forever bright, together in the dark.

The Light of Together

In the morning glow we rise,
Hand in hand, under bright skies.
With laughter ringing in the air,
Together we chase away despair.

Paths intertwine, a dance so sweet,
Our hearts beat fast, a joyful treat.
In the warmth of our bond, we shine,
Every moment, truly divine.

Through storms that whirl, we stand strong,
In unity, we belong.
Guided by love, our spirits soar,
Together forever, we'll explore.

As shadows fall, we hold the light,
Creating memories, sparkling bright.
In each other's eyes, we find our way,
The light of together, come what may.

With every dawn, new dreams arise,
Building a future beneath the skies.
In the tapestry of life we weave,
Together we love, together we believe.

Shared Warmth

In winter's chill, we gather near,
Sharing stories, spreading cheer.
A gentle fire, soft and bright,
Wrapping us in its warm light.

With every laugh, we spark a flame,
In the comfort, we feel the same.
Fingers entwined, hearts open wide,
In shared warmth, we find our guide.

Through seasons changing, time will flow,
Our bond will grow, the love will show.
In quiet moments, joy unfolds,
Shared warmth with stories untold.

When darkness falls and fears arise,
In each other's arms, we find ties.
A steady pulse, a heartbeat true,
Our shared warmth, the fire anew.

With every sunset, dreams take flight,
We face the future, hearts alight.
In this embrace, we'll never part,
Shared warmth forever in our heart.

Constellations of Companions

Beneath the stars, our bond is clear,
Constellations formed, drawing near.
Guided by lights that twinkle bright,
Companions through the endless night.

In laughter's echo, we find our guide,
Mapping dreams with friends by our side.
Through galaxies, we roam and play,
Constellations of love, come what may.

With every story, we paint the sky,
In this vast cosmos, we reach high.
Together we wander, hearts aligned,
Constellations of companions intertwined.

As planets spin and time goes on,
Our bond, a haven, always drawn.
With every hug, every shared smile,
We create magic, mile by mile.

And when the night seems dark and cold,
Our constellations, treasures untold.
Shining brighter than any star,
In this universe, we've come so far.

Flashes of Belonging

In the midst of chaos, we find our place,
Flashes of belonging, a warm embrace.
With every heartbeat, we spark a flame,
Together we rise, refusing blame.

Through whispers shared, we weave a thread,
Tales of adventures where we've led.
In laughter's glow, we break the night,
Flashes of belonging, pure delight.

With hands held tight, we weather the storm,
In this circle, we keep each other warm.
Through trials faced, our spirits strong,
Flashes of belonging, where we belong.

In every moment, our hearts ignite,
Crafting memories, taking flight.
Through time and space, forever true,
Flashes of belonging, me and you.

As sunsets fade and dawns arise,
In every glance, love never lies.
We stand united, bold and free,
In flashes of belonging, just you and me.

Beneath the Shared Stars

Under a blanket of night,
We weave our dreams with light.
Whispers carried by the breeze,
Two souls dancing with such ease.

Galaxies in our eyes shine,
Momentary, yet divine.
Constellations draw us near,
In this silence, we adhere.

The moon watches from above,
A witness to our soft love.
Together we find our place,
In this cosmic, warm embrace.

With each twinkle, heartbeats toll,
Connected, you are my soul.
Beneath the vast, endless skies,
Our love glimmers, never dies.

In the stillness of the night,
Your hand holds mine, feels so right.
Together, we share our scars,
Forever beneath the stars.

Flames of Understanding

In the hearth where passions glow,
We share the tales we both know.
From the embers, warmth does rise,
Building bridges, breaking lies.

Every flicker tells a tale,
Of heartaches faced yet we prevail.
With each spark, our truths ignite,
Lit by love, we conquer night.

Bound together by this fire,
We learn to trust, to aspire.
Fanning flames of empathy,
Creating depth, you and me.

With the heat, the shadows fade,
In this light, we're unafraid.
What once was dark now shines bright,
United we stand, hearts in flight.

In this dance of light and shade,
Strong foundations we have made.
Flames of understanding blaze,
In their warmth, our spirits raise.

Echoes of Laughter

In the garden of our dreams,
Laughter flows like joyous streams.
Every giggle, every cheer,
Echoes wide, we dance in here.

Moments shared, pure delight,
Turning darkness into light.
With each chuckle, fears abate,
In this joy, we celebrate.

The world fades, we're just us,
In this laughter, we find trust.
Joining voices in the air,
Happiness is everywhere.

Through the echoes, we grow strong,
In the rhythm, we belong.
Side by side, we chase the sun,
Laughing hearts, we are as one.

Time may pass, but laughter stays,
Guiding us through life's maze.
In those echoes, we take flight,
Finding comfort in the night.

Wings of Warmth

When the cold wraps around tight,
Your embrace is pure, so right.
With you, I find a safe place,
Wrapped in love's gentle grace.

Your smile lights up the gray sky,
With you always, I feel high.
Soft whispers brush across my skin,
In your arms, I feel the win.

Flying high on hope's embrace,
Together we create our space.
Wings of warmth wrapped around,
In your love, I am found.

Through the storms, we soar as one,
Our journey vast, just begun.
With each heartbeat, we take flight,
Guided by love's shining light.

With you, my spirit feels free,
In your heart, I long to be.
Together we glide through the air,
Wings of warmth, a love so rare.

The Warmth of Companionship

In gentle whispers, hearts entwine,
A bond unbroken, love divine.
With laughter shared, we feel so free,
Together we create our harmony.

Through storms we stand, side by side,
In every challenge, we take pride.
A warm embrace when days are tough,
In friendship's light, we find enough.

With every moment that we share,
A treasure grows, beyond compare.
Through trials faced and dreams pursued,
Companionship, our quietude.

Each memory made, a star will shine,
Illuminating paths that intertwine.
In silence, comfort; in chaos, cheer,
The warmth of you, forever near.

So let us wander, hand in hand,
In every moment, together we stand.
In the warmth of companionship, we find,
A love eternal, endlessly kind.

Coals of Loyalty

In darkest nights, a spark ignites,
A fire burns, its warmth invites.
Through trials faced, we stand our ground,
In loyalty's embrace, we are bound.

With every challenge, we grow strong,
Together, where we both belong.
The coals of trust, they never fade,
In storms of life, our bond is made.

Through years that pass, and winds that blow,
Our hearts like rivers, ever flow.
With whispered promises, we attest,
In loyalty found, we are blessed.

Through shadows cast and doubts that sway,
Our steadfast hearts will find the way.
A fiery glow, in darkest times,
Coals of loyalty, in rhythm and rhymes.

Together we rise, through thick and thin,
In unity found, we always win.
Through every trial, let our fires glow,
In the coals of loyalty, love will grow.

A Beacon of Support

In times of need, you're by my side,
A guiding light, my constant guide.
With open arms and listening ear,
A beacon of support, always near.

Through valleys low and mountains high,
You lift me up, you help me fly.
With every step, your strength I find,
A light that shines, forever kind.

In whispered doubts and fears that creep,
You plant a hope, in which I'll leap.
A shelter built, in storms we face,
With love as our unwavering grace.

Your laughter echoes, a joyful sound,
In every moment, I'm safely found.
Together we soar, with hearts so bold,
A beacon of support, like stories told.

So hand in hand, we walk this road,
In each other's hearts, we share the load.
With you beside me, I can explore,
A beacon of support, forevermore.

Kindred Spirits' Light

In quiet moments, our spirits blend,
Two souls united, forever friends.
With laughter shared and tears embraced,
In kindred light, our fears are chased.

Through whispered secrets and dreams we weave,
A tapestry bright, we both believe.
Together we dance through joy and strife,
In kindred spirits, we find our life.

With every heartbeat, a song we sing,
In harmony's grasp, our voices ring.
Through every challenge, we intertwine,
Kindred spirits, our souls align.

In shadows cast, we light the way,
With every word, our hearts will sway.
In moments cherished, we gain our sight,
In kindred spirits, we are the light.

So here's to the bond that we all share,
In every moment, precious and rare.
Together we shine, a radiant flight,
Two kindred spirits, igniting the night.

Ties that Spark

In the silence of the night,
Echoes softly call,
Whispers of a bond,
Together we stand tall.

Threads of fate entwined,
In moments shared,
Laughter like a song,
In hearts, love declared.

Through storms and through calm,
We find our way,
In the dance of life,
Forever we sway.

A glance, a smile shines,
Lighting up the grey,
In the warmth of you,
I choose to stay.

With every heartbeat,
Ties that won't break,
For in this journey,
It's love we make.

Illuminated Hearts

In the twilight's glow,
Hearts begin to ignite,
Radiance shared,
Their futures burn bright.

Like stars in the sky,
Each story unique,
In the depth of souls,
A connection we seek.

Through time's gentle flow,
Our spirits entwined,
Illuminated paths,
With love, we are blind.

In shadows we dance,
With courage, we spark,
Each step a reflection,
Of light in the dark.

Together we shine,
In moments divine,
Illuminated hearts,
Forever entwined.

The Fire of Connection

In the stillness of dawn,
Fires start to burn,
Embers of our past,
In every twist, we learn.

A glance ignites the flame,
A whisper draws near,
With each shared moment,
We conquer all fear.

In the heat of our truth,
We find our might,
Bound by the warmth,
In the depth of night.

Through laughter and tears,
The sparks will remain,
A forge of our love,
Through joy and pain.

Together we blaze,
No shadows in sight,
The fire of connection,
Guides us with light.

Unity's Radiance

In the fabric of time,
We weave our own thread,
Unity's embrace,
Where all hearts are led.

Hand in hand we stand,
Through the highs and lows,
In the rhythm of life,
Together it flows.

From mountains to seas,
Our spirits align,
In the bond we create,
True love will shine.

With hope in our hearts,
We conquer the dark,
Unity's radiance,
Ignites every spark.

As we journey on,
With courage and grace,
In unity's light,
We find our true place.

Flames of Memories Past

In the glow of twilight's embrace,
We gather shadows, lost in space.
Whispers linger in the air,
Echoes of laughter, a tender care.

Flickering lights dance in our minds,
Recollections of love, time unwinds.
Each ember a story, a tale to share,
Igniting the night, memories laid bare.

Through crackling fires, we find our peace,
In the warmth of the past, our hearts release.
Moments like stars, they twinkle bright,
Guiding our souls through the silent night.

With every flame, a story glows,
In the hearth of our hearts, it only grows.
We kindle the spark of days gone by,
As the night deepens, we watch and sigh.

Memories dance, a bittersweet song,
In the flames of our hearts, we find we belong.
Wrapped in nostalgia, together we stand,
In the warmth of remembrance, hand in hand.

The Warmth of Tomorrow

A rising sun breaks through the gray,
Casting shadows of yesterday.
Hope ignites with the morning light,
Promising dreams, futures bright.

Breezes carry whispers of chance,
Inviting hearts to join the dance.
In the glow of what's yet to be,
We find our place, we find the key.

With open arms, we greet the dawn,
Each moment a thread, a tapestry drawn.
In the journey forward, we learn to fly,
Letting go of fears as we touch the sky.

Together we weave a fabric of trust,
Nurtured by kindness, in hope we must.
From the ashes of doubt, we rise anew,
In the warmth of tomorrow, our dreams come true.

With every heartbeat, a chance to create,
In the dance of life, we celebrate fate.
Bound by a vision of what lies ahead,
In the warmth of tomorrow, our spirits are fed.

Light and Laughter Combined

In the garden where joy blooms bright,
Laughter dances, a pure delight.
Sunbeams play on petals fair,
Each moment treasured, light as air.

With every giggle, warmth ignites,
In the tapestry woven by days and nights.
A symphony played in harmony found,
Light and laughter, forever abound.

Through the valleys of life we roam,
In shared tales, we build our home.
Every chuckle, a memory spun,
A reminder that together we've won.

As stars twinkle in the velvet sky,
We cherish the moments that flutter by.
In the embrace of laughter, we find our song,
In the light of our hearts, where we all belong.

So let us gather, hand in hand,
In a world where love and joy stand.
In the light of laughter, spirits entwine,
Creating a tapestry, beautifully divine.

Threads of Light

Weaving colors with threads of grace,
In every stitch, a sacred space.
Threads of light binding our hearts,
Creating a canvas where love imparts.

Each moment a fiber, intricately spun,
In the tapestry of life, we all are one.
With each gentle pull, the pattern grows,
In the embrace of connection, our essence shows.

Through the weave of time, we find our way,
In the light of friendship, brighter each day.
Threads of laughter, bonds intertwine,
Crafting a future, brilliantly divine.

As the loom of life continues to turn,
In the fires of passion, our spirits burn.
With every heartbeat, a thread we spin,
In the dance of creation, we all begin.

So let us cherish each precious thread,
In the light of our love, let joy be spread.
Together we weave, in harmony bright,
Crafting a world from threads of light.

Threads of Light

In the dawn's gentle glow, we weave,
Threads of gold that softly cleave,
Binding moments, sweet and bright,
Whispers of love, threads of light.

Through the shadows, we will glide,
With every heartbeat, side by side,
Stitching hopes in patterns tight,
Together we craft, threads of light.

Memories dance in the air,
Each a story, sweet and rare,
Flickering softly, pure delight,
Colorful dreams, threads of light.

In the twilight, we will find,
Patterns etched within the mind,
Guiding us through the night,
Ever shining, threads of light.

As the stars begin to rise,
We'll unravel, learn, and prize,
Every moment, joyous flight,
Tangled softly, threads of light.

In the Heart's Hearth

In the heart's warm, glowing space,
Memories gather, time's embrace,
Fires flicker, shadows play,
This is where our dreams will stay.

Laughter echoes, stories unfold,
Embers whisper, secrets told,
Each heartbeat sings, a soft ballet,
In the heart's hearth, love's array.

Comfort found in every glance,
Magic woven in our dance,
Through the night, we light the way,
In the heart's hearth, we will stay.

Hope ignites with every spark,
Lighting paths within the dark,
Together, we chase fears away,
In the heart's hearth, come what may.

With you here, I am complete,
Every moment feels so sweet,
Life's embrace, a warm display,
In the heart's hearth, forever play.

Fireside Tales of Us

By the fire, warmth ignites,
Sharing whispers, cozy nights,
Tales of love and laughter shared,
Each moment cherished, always cared.

Shadows dance upon the wall,
Echoing laughter, soft and small,
Stories woven, hearts entwined,
Fireside tales of us combined.

Every flicker, memory's spark,
Holding close each cherished mark,
In these tales, our souls align,
Fireside stories, pure divine.

With each ember, dreams will grow,
In the glow, our hearts will know,
From the past, we find our trust,
Fireside tales, love is a must.

As the night begins to fade,
In the warmth, our promise made,
Together strong, in love we trust,
Fireside tales of us, a must.

Blazing Trails Through Life

Onward we go, blazing trails,
Through wild woods and gentle gales,
Hand in hand, we rise and roam,
In every step, we make a home.

Mountains high and valleys deep,
Through the storms, our promise keep,
With each sunrise, we unite,
Blazing trails through life, our light.

Paths unknown will guide our way,
Adventure calls, we cannot stay,
With every heartbeat, every fight,
In nature's arms, we find delight.

Through the forest, whispers call,
With your spirit, I stand tall,
In this journey, love ignites,
Blazing trails through life, our sights.

In every turn and twist we make,
Building memories, life's great stake,
Together onward, hearts so bright,
Blazing trails through life, our right.

The Warmth of Laughter

In the glow of a bright sun,
We gather as friends in cheer,
With laughter that dances,
It lightens each burden here.

Echoes of joy surround,
A symphony of sweet delight,
Every chuckle a treasure,
A moment that feels just right.

Hearts open like flowers,
In each shared, gentle jest,
A bond forged in humor,
To feel truly blessed.

Through storms and through trials,
Together we'll stand tall,
With laughter as our armor,
In joy, we will not fall.

So let the laughter linger,
In memories we hold dear,
For in the warmth of laughter,
Love's essence shines so clear.

Flickering Moments

Time dances on the edge,
Of fleeting, soft hours,
Each flicker a reminder,
Of life's precious powers.

In twilight's gentle kiss,
We find whispers of grace,
Moments that hold us close,
In a warm, sweet embrace.

The candle's soft glow sings,
Of dreams and of hopes,
As shadows weave stories,
In life's rich tapestry ropes.

We gather these fragments,
Each spark like a star,
Illuminating our path,
No matter how far.

Through flickering moments,
Together we will roam,
Discovering life's magic,
In the heart, we find home.

The Audacity of Light

In the darkness, a spark glows,
A bold burst of bright flare,
Challenging shadows deep,
With its unwavering glare.

It dances across the night,
Defying the weighty gloom,
A herald of hope's whispers,
In the quiet, it blooms.

The audacity of light shines,
Filling hearts with its grace,
Guiding the wayward,
To a clearer, safer space.

Each dawn brings its embrace,
A promise of new dreams,
Illuminating our paths,
In its radiant beams.

So let the light rise fierce,
Through valleys and through heights,
For within its bold essence,
We find courage in our flights.

Kindled Connections

In the warmth of shared stories,
We find our spirits unite,
Every word a bridge built,
In the soft glow of night.

Hands clasped in understanding,
Eyes meeting in trust,
In the dance of connections,
We find love is a must.

With laughter and whispers,
We kindle the spark,
Nurturing the tender flame,
In the depths of the dark.

These bonds are our treasures,
Jewels shining so bright,
In every little moment,
Our hearts take flight.

So let's cherish this journey,
With every heartfelt glance,
For in kindled connections,
We find our shared dance.

Radiant Connections

In the stillness of the night,
Two hearts glow, a gentle light.
Whispers weave through the dark,
With every spark, a tender mark.

Hands entwined, they find their way,
Navigating night and day.
A bond built on silent grace,
In every smile, a warm embrace.

Rays of hope in laughter rise,
Reflecting dreams in each other's eyes.
The paths they walk, side by side,
In radiant truth, they confide.

Through storms of doubt and trials faced,
Together, fears are surely erased.
A journey shared, the sweetest song,
In connections deep, they belong.

As time flows like a gentle stream,
In every moment, they find their dream.
With every heartbeat, lifetime spent,
In radiant joy, their souls are sent.

Flames of Trust

In the shadow's soft embrace,
Two souls ignite, a sacred space.
With every word, a kindled flame,
In the hush, they weave their name.

Through the flicker, secrets shared,
Each confession shows they cared.
A fire born from honest tears,
In honest whispers, no more fears.

As time unfolds, this flame won't cease,
In warmth, they find their peace.
Trust ignites with every glance,
In the dance of a trusted chance.

Together they rise, a brilliant blaze,
In the dark, their light stays.
As embers glow, they move as one,
In flames of trust, new lives begun.

The Light We Carry

In the dawn of a brand new day,
With steadfast hearts, we find our way.
Each step forward, a beacon bright,
In shadows cast, we are the light.

Through storms that come, through skies so gray,
We stand united, come what may.
With every laugh, with every tear,
We forge a bond that knows no fear.

The light we carry, it shines so clear,
Illuminating paths we hold dear.
In moments shared, in whispers low,
We nurture the flame, let it grow.

In the depth of night, we will not part,
For you hold the light within your heart.
Together we shine, a radiant pair,
In this journey, we're meant to share.

Souls Uniting in Warmth

Beneath the stars, a quiet glow,
Two hearts meld, as breezes flow.
In gentle sighs, whispers blend,
A sacred dance that will not end.

As laughter fills the evening air,
With every glance, a deeper care.
In the warmth of a shared embrace,
Souls unite in a timeless space.

Hands held tight, through night so still,
With every pulse, they share their will.
In this moment, a bond so strong,
Their hearts sing an eternal song.

Through every challenge, they stand bold,
In the warmth, their truth unfolds.
Together they rise, spirits aglow,
In unison, love's vibrant flow.

As dawn approaches, light will break,
In every heartbeat, love awakes.
Together forging memories warm,
In souls uniting, forever transformed.

A Flicker of Understanding

In the silence, thoughts collide,
A soft glow ignites the night.
Words unspoken, yet we know,
In shared glances, hearts take flight.

Beneath the stars, we sit and breathe,
Unraveled dreams, we both perceive.
With every sigh, a bond is spun,
Two souls, as one, we gently run.

The shadows fade, our fears recede,
A flicker grows, we plant the seed.
Through trials faced, and laughter shared,
In this moment, love is declared.

In whispers soft, the world dissolves,
Our understanding gently evolves.
Though words may fail, our spirits unite,
Flickering flames, we find our light.

With open hearts, we tread this path,
In this dance, we find our math.
A flicker spreads, a gentle spark,
Together we walk, no fear of dark.

Together We Illuminate

In shadows deep, we find our way,
With hands held tight, come what may.
Light shines brighter, side by side,
Together we fight, love as our guide.

In laughter shared, the days unfold,
Through whispered dreams, our stories told.
With each heartbeat, the distance fades,
Together we glow like twilight glades.

A candle flickers, a beacon strong,
In this embrace, we both belong.
Together we rise, and fears subside,
In your warmth, my heart confides.

With every step, the path is clear,
In harmony sweet, you draw me near.
Together we weave, a tapestry grand,
Illuminate the dark, hand in hand.

The journey stretches, horizons wide,
With trust and love, we turn the tide.
Together we stand, the world aglow,
In unity bright, our spirits flow.

Coals of Companionship

In the quiet, embers gleam,
Warmth of laughter, like a dream.
Coals of friendship burn so bright,
Even in dark, we find our light.

Through storms we dance, in rain we play,
With every step, we find our way.
Fanning the flames, we share our fears,
In every glance, we dry our tears.

The hearth we build, through thick and thin,
In moments lost, together we win.
Coals that fade, we stoke anew,
With every memory, our bond rings true.

In quiet nights, and busy days,
Together we walk through life's maze.
With hearts ablaze, we chase the night,
In the coals of love, we'll find our flight.

So hold me close, let time stand still,
In the warmth of us, we both shall fill.
Coals of companionship burn eternal,
In this embrace, our hearts turn infernal.

The Hearth of Our Hearts

In the corner, the fire glows,
With every spark, affection grows.
The hearth of our hearts, safe and warm,
In your presence, I find my calm.

Through seasons change, our love remains,
In joy and sorrow, through losses and gains.
Together we build this sacred space,
In the hearth of our hearts, we find our place.

With morning light, we greet the day,
In shared moments, we laugh and sway.
Together we share the simplest art,
In the warmth and glow that fills the heart.

Each crackle tells a tale of grace,
In the memories made, we both embrace.
The hearth a symbol of what we share,
In love's quiet dance, we know we're rare.

So gather 'round, let the flames rise,
In the warmth of us, the world complies.
The hearth of our hearts will never tire,
Together we flourish, forever inspired.

The Song of Sparks

In shadows deep, the embers dance,
A flicker bright, a timeless chance.
The night ignites with whispers low,
As sparks take flight, they gleam and glow.

They twirl and weave a tale anew,
In every crackle, stories brew.
A symphony of light and air,
In fleeting moments, joy laid bare.

From hearth and home, the warmth spreads wide,
Together here, let hearts abide.
Through every spark, a bond is drawn,
A dance of fire, from dusk till dawn.

Emblazed in night, the world ignites,
In the gentle hum of fleeting lights.
With each bright burst, our spirits soar,
In every spark, we long for more.

So let us gather, hand in hand,
To share the glow, to understand.
For in this song of sparks we find,
The threads of love that intertwine.

Light of Each Other

In quiet shimmers, shadows fade,
Two souls converge, a bond is made.
With every glance, the world ignites,
In love's embrace, all wrongs feel right.

Through trials faced and laughter shared,
The light of each, the other cared.
In darkest hours, we still find gold,
A treasure chest of love untold.

Your eyes reflect the stars above,
A universe that speaks of love.
In gentle moments, gold unspun,
Together we are more than one.

For in this glow, we shine more bright,
Two hearts aflame, dispelling night.
Together brave, we face what's near,
In every dawn, you are my cheer.

So let us cherish, side by side,
In every trial, in every tide.
For in the light of each we find,
The boundless gift of hearts aligned.

The Glow of Memories

Upon the walls, the moments gleam,
In woven tales, we dare to dream.
Each snapshot warm, each laugh a thread,
In the fabric of time, we are wed.

Through golden hues, the past calls forth,
In silent whispers, our true worth.
With every glance at days gone by,
We find our joy beneath the sky.

The glow of memories, sweet and bright,
A beacon soft in the darkest night.
With every heartbeat, stories flow,
Together etched in time's gentle glow.

In laughter shared and tears once shed,
In places touched and words once said.
A tapestry of love unfurls,
In every thread, our life whirls.

So let us hold what we have known,
In every moment, love has grown.
For in these glimmers, we find grace,
In-memory's glow, we embrace space.

Swirling Flames of Joy

Amidst the night, the flames do dance,
A joyous spark, a fleeting chance.
In swirling colors, hearts take flight,
With each warm flicker, pure delight.

The fire speaks in crackling tunes,
With laughter bright beneath the moons.
As embers rise and twirl so free,
We join the rhythm, you and me.

In every swirl, the joy expands,
With open hearts, with open hands.
Through warmth and light, we share the glow,
In flaming circles, love will grow.

So come, my dear, let's sway and spin,
With every flame, a dance begins.
In swirling flames, we find our place,
With each heartbeat, our spirits grace.

For in the warmth of joyous fire,
We rise together, climbing higher.
In every moment, memories blend,
In swirling flames, our lives transcend.

Together We Burn Bright

In the night we find our spark,
Illuminating shadows dark.
Our dreams like flames entwine,
Together we will shine.

With laughter that ignites the air,
We conquer fears, we boldly dare.
Side by side we face the test,
Together, we know we're blessed.

Each moment shared, a precious time,
In symphonies of hearts, we rhyme.
Together, spirits soaring high,
Like stars that kiss the sky.

In the warmth of kindred souls,
We stitch together fragile roles.
With every pulse, our fires grow,
In unity, we let love flow.

And when the world feels cold and gray,
We'll find a way, come what may.
In the light that we create,
Together, we celebrate.

A Warm Embrace

In the stillness of the night,
I find comfort in your light.
With open arms that draw me near,
Your warmth chases away my fear.

The whispers soft, like gentle breeze,
In your embrace, my heart finds peace.
With every sigh, and every glance,
We weave together our sweet dance.

The world outside may feel so cold,
Yet in your arms, love's tales unfold.
Like blankets wrapped on winter's eve,
In you, I find the strength to believe.

With every heartbeat, time stands still,
In the embrace that bends my will.
A sanctuary built for two,
Forever cherished, warm and true.

So keep me close, don't let me go,
In this warmth, our love will grow.
For in your hold, the world feels right,
With you, my heart takes flight.

The Glow of Old Friends

Through the years, we've walked this road,
In laughter shared, our stories flowed.
The glow of youth, now seasoned light,
In friendship's warmth, our souls take flight.

We've weathered storms, we've climbed the hills,
With every joy, and every thrill.
In whispered secrets, trust we find,
Bound by memories intertwined.

Each moment captured in our hearts,
From distant past, we never part.
With ties that time cannot erase,
In every smile, a familiar face.

So here we stand, in twilight's hue,
With every laugh, we'll start anew.
The glow of old friends, shining bright,
In their embrace, there's pure delight.

Together, we'll face the dawn's embrace,
In the book of life, we leave our trace.
In this tapestry, forever spun,
The glow of friendship shines like the sun.

The Lantern's Light

A lantern flickers in the night,
Guiding souls with gentle light.
Through shadows thick, it holds the way,
A beacon bright at close of day.

Each flame a story, tales untold,
Of dreams and hopes, of hearts so bold.
In its glow, we gather near,
Together banishing all fear.

When paths grow dark and stars are few,
The lantern shines, a promise true.
With every flicker, one might find,
The warmth that lingers, two entwined.

In its embrace, shadows retreat,
A moment shared, a love replete.
We chase the doubts, we chase the night,
With the lantern's glow, we find our light.

So carry on, and hold it tight,
Together we'll brave the darkest night.
With every step, we stand as one,
In the lantern's light, our journey's begun.

Illuminating Shadows

In the stillness of the night,
Shadows play and dance bright,
Whispers echo through the trees,
Caught in gentle evening's breeze.

Moonlight weaves a silken thread,
Casting dreams where shadows tread,
They flicker soft, then fade away,
Drawn by dawn's first golden ray.

In the corners dark they loom,
Glimmers of forgotten bloom,
Stories of what once was known,
In the silence, seeds are sown.

Through each shadow, light will weave,
Tales of hope we still believe,
From the depths, a truth must rise,
Shining bright in midnight skies.

In the quiet, find your peace,
Let the shadows slowly cease,
Feel the warmth as daylight breaks,
In the light, the heart awakes.

Touches of Warmth

Morning sun upon the ground,
Softest rays in silence found,
Warmth that kisses skin so light,
Bringing forth a brand new sight.

Gentle breezes softly sway,
In the garden where we play,
Every petal, every leaf,
Whispers tales of sweet belief.

Golden hours, time at ease,
Wrap us in their sweet embrace,
Moments shared, a giggle bright,
As the stars return at night.

Hearts ignite like summer's glow,
In the warmth, our spirits flow,
Hands held tight through trials we face,
Finding strength in love's embrace.

With each touch, a story starts,
Crafting beats from tender hearts,
Together in this dance we sway,
Finding warmth in every day.

Flames of Inspiration

In the hearth where embers gleam,
Burns a long-forgotten dream,
Fuel the fire, let it rise,
Ignite the spark of your own skies.

Flickers dance with rhymes untold,
In their warmth, the brave grow bold,
Chasing shadows, crafting light,
With each breath, set thoughts alight.

Ideas soar like fireflies,
Painting hopes in vivid skies,
Each flame a path we dare to tread,
Guiding all those visions fed.

Challenge boundaries, break each chain,
In the flames, there is no pain,
Fuel your passion, let it grow,
From the ashes, new seeds sow.

Let the fire spark your soul,
In its warmth, you will be whole,
For in inspiration's dance,
Lives a key, a timeless chance.

The Firekeeper's Heart

In the shadows, secrets dwell,
A firekeeper breathes and swells,
Keeping watch through night and day,
Guarding flames that dance and sway.

Kindling warmth with tender care,
Heart aflame, a love laid bare,
With each flicker, stories told,
Of brave souls, both fierce and bold.

Through the trials, storms may rage,
But the fire will not disengage,
In the heart, a steady beat,
Carving paths that none defeat.

Gather 'round, feel safe and sound,
In the shelter, light is found,
Embers whisper, softly sing,
Promises of hopeful spring.

In the keeper's watchful gaze,
Lives a warmth that ever stays,
For a heart that truly cares,
Is the flame that ever dares.

Our Shared Radiance

In the morning light we rise,
Sharing dreams beneath the skies.
Together we chase the sun,
In this dance, we are as one.

Through the shadows, warmth we find,
Lifting hearts, our souls aligned.
Every smile a gentle spark,
Guiding us through the dark.

With each step, a bond so bright,
Filling the world with pure delight.
In laughter, our voices blend,
A melody that will not end.

In moments, both big and small,
Our shared radiance embraces all.
No journey too tough to face,
When together, we find our place.

As the stars twinkle above,
We reflect all that is love.
In unity, our spirits soar,
Lighting paths forevermore.

The Glow of Together

Hand in hand, we walk the lane,
Facing joys and sharing pain.
With each word, the warmth we share,
A glow that lingers in the air.

In quiet times, in laughter's song,
Together, we know we belong.
Every moment, a treasured gift,
In each other, our spirits lift.

Through storms that try to blur our sight,
We find our way, igniting light.
The bond we hold, a precious thread,
Woven with love, where hearts are led.

As dusk falls, our dreams align,
In the glow, our spirits shine.
Every heartbeat sings and sways,
Together, we light our days.

With shadows cast and stars aglow,
Our friendship blooms, a lovely flow.
In the tapestry of time we weave,
The glow of together, we believe.

In the Heat of Friendship

Through trials deep, we stand our ground,
In the heat, true strength is found.
With laughter bright and spirits free,
Friendship blooms like the tallest tree.

When the skies are filled with gray,
We chase the clouds, make them sway.
In every challenge, hand in hand,
Together, we always stand.

The warmth of trust, a flame that burns,
In each embrace, the heart returns.
Through laughter shared and tears that grace,
In the heat, we find our place.

Each story told, a thread that binds,
With every memory, hope unwinds.
In our hearts, a bond so true,
In the heat of friendship, me and you.

So let us dance 'neath the blazing sun,
In the warmth of laughter, we have won.
With each moment, bright like gold,
In the heat of friendship, we are bold.

The Illuminated Path

In the dim light where shadows play,
We find the bliss in our own way.
With every step, a whisper heard,
The illuminated path, love's sweet word.

Through the forest of dreams we chase,
Finding joy in every space.
With hearts aglow, we walk with grace,
Hand in hand, we embrace this place.

Each twist and turn, a lesson learned,
The light within us ever burned.
Together we soar, the limits fade,
On this path, our fears evade.

As night falls softly, stars ignite,
Guiding us through the tender night.
With hope and love, we stay in stride,
On this illuminated guide.

In the journey, shadows will fall,
Yet our light will conquer all.
With every laugh, and every tear,
The illuminated path draws near.

The Bonfire of Belonging

In the flicker of night's embrace,
Laughter dances, shadows trace.
Voices blend in joyful song,
Hearts unite, where we belong.

The warmth around, a sacred space,
Memories held in gentle grace.
Stories shared by the fire's glow,
Together, we let our spirits flow.

Each flame a whisper of the past,
Bonding moments, meant to last.
With every spark, connection grows,
In this circle, love clearly shows.

As embers fade, our bonds ignite,
Kindred souls in this starry night.
Through trials faced, we forge our way,
Together we thrive, come what may.

So gather close, feel the heat,
In this bonfire, our lives complete.
A place where hearts can truly sing,
In the glow of belonging, we take wing.

A Radiant Journey

Beneath the vast and shining sky,
We take our steps, just you and I.
With every turn, a new surprise,
Together, we chase horizons wide.

The road ahead, both dark and bright,
Guided by stars, we find our light.
With laughter echoing on the breeze,
We embrace the wonders, hearts at ease.

Mountains rise and rivers flow,
In every moment, love will grow.
Hand in hand, through thick and thin,
With faith in each other, we begin.

As dawn breaks forth with golden hues,
We paint our dreams with vibrant views.
In every challenge, every cheer,
Our radiant journey shines so clear.

And at the end, when the day is done,
We'll look back at all we have won.
Two souls entwined, forever free,
In this journey, just you and me.

Steadfast in the Glow

In the silence of the night so still,
A gentle warmth begins to fill.
Through storms and trials, we hold tight,
Our hearts aglow, shining bright.

With each new dawn, we rise again,
Facing fears, the joy, the pain.
In every struggle, hand in hand,
Our steadfast love will always stand.

Moments cherished, souls entwined,
In the glow, our hearts reminded.
Through whispered dreams and softest sighs,
Together we reach for the skies.

With each heartbeat, every breath,
We conquer shadows, conquer death.
In the warmth of love's embrace,
We find our truth in this sacred space.

And as the stars begin to fade,
We hold the magic that we've made.
In life's journey, come what may,
We're steadfast in the glow—always.

Luminescent Bonds

In the dance of light, we find our way,
Through shadowed paths of night and day.
With every step, our hearts align,
Luminescent bonds, forever shine.

The whispers of the past still flow,
In the warmth, our spirits grow.
Through trials faced, we rise anew,
Bound by love, forever true.

Each moment shared, a treasure rare,
In laughter's echoes, we lay bare.
Through tangled paths, we pave our road,
Our hearts connect, lightening the load.

In the tapestry of time we weave,
With threads of hope, we dare believe.
Together strong, we'll weather the storm,
In luminescent bonds, we transform.

So here we stand, hand in hand,
In a world where dreams expand.
With every heartbeat, love will grow,
In luminescent light, we glow.

Warmth in the Shadows

In the quiet night's embrace,
Whispers dance with the breeze,
Soft glow from ancient stones,
Embers glowing with ease.

A flicker of light bites deep,
Casting shapes on the wall,
Memories wrapped in the night,
As shadows rise and fall.

Together we find our way,
Through the dark, hand in hand,
Every heartbeat a promise,
In this enchanted land.

The stories we softly weave,
Echoes of love and hope,
Within the shadows we stand,
Learning how to cope.

Here in the warmth of dreams,
Hearts ignite pure delight,
Together we'll face the stars,
In this magical night.

Whispered Secrets in the Firelight

In the crackle of the flames,
Secrets softly are shared,
Each spark a whisper of dreams,
In the night, unprepared.

The shadows dance with delight,
As stories come alive,
We lean closer, breath held tight,
In this warmth, we thrive.

Fingers trace the glowing lines,
Drawing maps on the floor,
Each glow a path that shines,
We open up, explore.

With laughter dipping low,
Like embers floating free,
Our hearts, a gentle glow,
A tapestry, just we.

As the world fades away,
We hold the moment still,
In firelight's soft sway,
Our spirits gently fill.

Illuminated Souls

In the depth of night, we glow,
Guided by radiant dreams,
Every soul, a soft light show,
Dancing like silver beams.

Together we carve the night,
With laughter, love, and grace,
Each step a chance to ignite,
This wild, wondrous space.

Our secrets ignite the air,
In whispers softly spread,
Like stars we rise, we dare,
Illuminated, no dread.

With every shared embrace,
The darkness starts to fade,
In the heart's sacred place,
A promise never made.

In our glow, we find peace,
Sparking joy's lively fight,
Together, we seek release,
From shadows into light.

The Glow of Shared Laughter

In the stillness of the night,
Laughter blooms like spring,
With echoes that take flight,
And joy we freely bring.

Each chuckle warms the air,
As smiles dance in the dark,
Every moment we share,
Leaves behind a sweet mark.

Around the flickering flame,
Our hearts feel light and free,
In this glow, none feels shame,
Just pure, wild harmony.

Every story, every jest,
Forms a bridge, hand to hand,
In laughter, we feel blessed,
As we together stand.

With each spark that ignites,
A connection deep and true,
In our bonded delights,
The glow shines bright in you.

Glow of Endless Moments

In the whispers of the night,
Soft and shimmering stars alight.
Time drifts gently through our hands,
Moments cherished, love expands.

Every heartbeat, every glance,
Glimmers caught in timeless dance.
Endless echoes, laughter near,
In this glow, you are my cheer.

Seasons change, yet here we stand,
Together, side by side, unplanned.
Captured in the soft embrace,
Memories held in time and space.

Through the shadows, brightness flows,
Lighting paths where love bestows.
In your eyes, the universe glows,
Endless moments, how love grows.

So let us paint the night sky bright,
With colors born from pure delight.
In this endless, radiant space,
You and I, forever face to face.

Flames of Support

In the silence, a spark ignites,
Fueling dreams on starry nights.
When the world feels dark and cold,
Together, we are brave and bold.

Through the storms, we hold our ground,
In your strength, my hope I've found.
Hand in hand, we rise anew,
With every challenge, I believe in you.

United voices, spirits soar,
In the battles, we want more.
Each flame a promise, shining bright,
Guiding us through every plight.

In laughter's warmth or sorrow's weight,
Side by side, we navigate.
With every step, our hearts align,
In this journey, your light is mine.

Through the years, unwavering glow,
Our bond, a force the world can't know.
With flames of support, we'll ignite,
The path ahead, forever bright.

Ashes and Affection

In the ember's fading light,
Whispers linger soft and slight.
From the ashes, love will rise,
Blooming softly where hope lies.

Through the trials, we have grown,
In the fire, seeds of love sown.
Through the pain, we've found our grace,
In each other, a safe place.

Tears may fall, yet hearts will mend,
In the heat, our spirits blend.
In every wound, a lesson learned,
From the flames, a fire yearned.

With gentle hands, we mold the past,
Turning ruins into warmth that lasts.
Through ashes of what once has been,
A new beginning waits within.

So rise we must, like phoenixes proud,
In the glow of affection, shout loud.
For even in darkness, we have seen,
Love's the thread that weaves the dream.

Interwoven Lights

Beneath the vast and starry dome,
Our hearts entwined, we find a home.
Threads of laughter, whispers gentle,
In this tapestry, love is central.

Golden rays and midnight hues,
Each color blooms with vibrant views.
With every moment, hearts ignite,
In the woven strands of pure delight.

Hand in hand, we journey through,
Paths illuminated, just me and you.
With every twist, a story's told,
In interwoven lights, we are bold.

Through the seasons, bright and dim,
A dance of shadows, love's sweet hymn.
United souls, forever bright,
Shining together, hearts take flight.

So let us gather every thread,
In this fabric where love is spread.
Interwoven, side by side,
In each other's warmth, we confide.

Kindred Hearts in the Embers

In the glow of fading light,
Two souls dance through the night,
With whispers soft and sweet,
Their pulse, a rhythmic beat.

Fires flicker, shadows play,
As hearts find their way,
In the warmth, they reside,
Together, they won't hide.

The embers speak their truth,
Of cherished love and youth,
In silent vows, they'll bind,
A peace that's hard to find.

Through storms and gentle rains,
Their bond remains, sustains,
In every tear and smile,
They walk the endless mile.

For kindred hearts ignite,
In the quiet of the night,
Together, they will mend,
A journey without end.

Sparks that Bind Us

From a spark, a flame can grow,
With whispers, soft and low,
What once was just a fable,
Now sits at the heart's stable.

Through every laugh and sigh,
In moments passing by,
A thread of gold will weave,
In love, we choose to believe.

Underneath the starry sky,
We shall laugh, we shall cry,
In the warmth of each embrace,
We find our sacred space.

Even when the world feels cold,
Our bond shines, brave and bold,
Through the trials we withstand,
Together we will stand.

The sparks that bind us here,
Are fueled by hope and cheer,
In each heartbeat, we trust,
Our love is strong, it must.

The Radiance of Togetherness

In the morning's gentle light,
We find joy in our sight,
Every moment intertwined,
A treasure we must find.

Through the laughter, through the tears,
We embrace all our fears,
With hands held tight in trust,
In our love, we combust.

The radiance that we share,
Reflects in the open air,
With every heartbeat's song,
Together, we belong.

Through the seasons, we shall roam,
In each other, we find home,
With warmth that lights the way,
We revel in each day.

For in unity, we thrive,
Always feeling so alive,
In every glance, we see,
This love was meant to be.

Ignite the Bond

In the depths of every soul,
There lies a shared goal,
To spark the flame within,
Where our journey can begin.

Each moment brings us near,
In laughter, in the tear,
Together, we ignite,
A glow that feels so right.

From ashes, rise anew,
With every shared view,
We discover what we seek,
In love, we grow unique.

With winds that may collide,
We'll stand side by side,
For every step we take,
In unity, we wake.

So let us fan the flame,
And never be the same,
For in each bond that's formed,
A legacy is warmed.